REJOICE

WHEN

YOU

DIE

THE NEW ORLEANS JAZZ FUNERALS

REJOICE
WHEN
YOU
DIE

PHOTOGRAPHS BY
LEO TOUCHET

TEXT BY
VERNEL BAGNERIS

INTRODUCTION BY
ELLIS L. MARSALIS, JR.

LOUISIANA STATE UNIVERSITY PRESS
Baton Rouge

Manufactured in Hong Kong

First printing

07 06 05 04 03 02 01 00 99 98 5 4 3 2 1

Designer: *a m k*

Typeface: *Garamond*

Printer and binder: *Everbest Printing Co. through Four Colour Imports, Ltd.,*

Louisville, Kentucky

Library of Congress Cataloging-in-Publication Data:

Touchet, Leo.

   Rejoice when you die : the New Orleans jazz funerals / photographs

by Leo Touchet ; introduction by Ellis L. Marsalis, Jr. ; text by Vernel

Bagneris.

      p. cm.

   ISBN 0-8071-2281-5 (cloth : alk. paper)

   ISBN 0-8071-2311-0 (spec. ed.)

   1. Funeral rites and cermonies—Louisiana—New Orleans—Pictorial

works. 2. Jazz musicians—Louisiana—New Orleans—Death—Pictorial

works. 3. Bands (Music)—Louisiana—New Orleans—Pictorial works.

I. Bagneris, Vernel. II. Title.

GT3211.N4T68 1998

393'.1'0976335—dc21   97-46450

The paper in this book meets the guidelines for permanence and durability of the Committee

on Production Guidelines for Book Longevity of the Council on Library Resources. ⊚

To Lydia Ann Smith

Her inspiration made these photographs possible.

♪

CONTENTS

by

LEO TOUCHET

I GREW up in Abbeville, Louisiana, in the 1940s and 1950s. I lived in the heart of Acadiana, as the Cajun area of Louisiana is known, among the tall oaks laden with Spanish moss, the pecan trees, rice and sugarcane fields, marshes, swamps lined with beautiful cypress coves, and bayous lined with pirogues. We gathered oysters and shrimp from the coastal bays. We fished for catfish, redfish, crawfish, sac-à-lait, and choupique. We hunted ducks, geese, poules d'eau, deer, rabbits, squirrels, alligators, and frogs. The foods we ate had names like filé gumbo, jambalaya, couche-couche, boudin, graton, courtbouillion, shrimp fricassée, maque-chou, crawfish étouffée, sauce piquant, pintade, and oreilles de cochon.

Cajun French was the language of my grandparents and my parents. They listened to the news in French on radio station KROF. Most of my more than two hundred aunts, uncles, and cousins lived in or near Abbeville. Their names were Clodise, Enolia, Loria, Lovelace, Lucien, Olita, Ursin, Ursule, and Zulma. Their family names became Boudreaux, Chauvin, Dubois, Hebert, LeBlanc, LeBoeuf, Melebeck, Primeaux, and Reaux. My role models were the carpenters, painters, plumbers, farmers, fishermen, fur trappers, and other hard-working Cajuns. They taught me to have pride in my work, and they gave me that wonderful *joie de vivre* with which to enjoy all that life has to offer.

Abbeville was still part of the segregated South. The blacks had separate churches, schools, swimming pools, rest rooms, and drinking fountains. The Cajuns had their *fais-do-do* where they played their fiddles and accordions and sang songs like *La Jolie Blonde, La Valse de Basile,* and *Allons à Grand Gueydan.* The French-speaking blacks in the area had zydeco (the name derives from *les haricots* in the song *Les Haricots sont pas salé),* a blues-based form of Cajun music played in nearby clubs that whites would not attend. Words like *Creole* and *jazz* were still way off into my future. Way off in New Orleans.

For most Cajuns at that time, New Orleans didn't even have a name. It was known to me simply as "en ville" (in the city), and people from outside Acadiana were known as "les Américains." Because of politics and politicians like Governor Earl K. Long and Abbeville's Dudley J. LeBlanc (better known as "Cousin Dud," the inventor of the patent medicine Hadacol), the state capital of Baton Rouge was better known to me than New Orleans.

In the early 1960s I moved to New Orleans for the first time. Integration was beginning to change the city and the South. The signs for separate rest rooms and water fountains for the "colored" were coming down. The public schools were in the early, violent stages of integration. At the Absinthe House Bar, the racist cabaret comedy *Nobody Likes a Smart Ass* was adding new lines with each federal court ruling. The restaurants and bars were facing the inevitability of white waiters having to serve black customers.

I would take my daughter Carolyn fishing at the Lake Pontchartrain levee. My son Patrick was born at Touro Infirmary. The Bourbon House was alive with an assortment of artists, writers, poets, and alcoholics. Tennessee Williams drank and socialized there. I drank there. The sidewalk artists from Jackson Square kept warm in the bar in the winter. Leo Meiersdorff, the great painter of jazz scenes, arrived in New Orleans, shared my house, and produced many of his paintings on my living room floor.

New Orleans was like a giant decadent magnet that kept drawing me back. I had to get back there every so often, simply to loosen the screws in my head (creatively speaking, of course). The city and the French Quarter have always stimulated me in my work and in my life, but I knew that if I stayed there too long, I'd lose those screws permanently.

In 1965, I became a photographer. I worked as a photojournalist in Southeast Asia and other parts of the world before returning to New Orleans in 1968. The movie *Live and Let Die,* which included a jazz funeral scene, popularized the jazz funerals and started attracting tourists and television coverage. The attention changed the nature of the traditional funerals and turned them into "happenings."

I photographed the people on the streets of New Orleans as a free-lance photojournalist for *Life* magazine, the *New York Times,* and other publications. I was teamed with great reporters such as David Chandler, Roy Reed, and Martin "Moe" Waldron. We covered the antiwar/free-love society and social activism along with the changes brought on by the movement. We documented the Jim Garrison versus Clay Shaw conspiracy trial, in which, we all felt, Garrison ruined the life of a perfectly innocent friend of ours. We reported on the environmental damage to the Atchafalaya Swamp caused by the U.S. Army Corps of Engineers. The Atchafalaya Basin Swamp, home to the Louisiana heron, the snowy egret, the Louisiana iris, and some of the best bass and sac-à-lait fishing in the world, is the largest river basin swamp in the United States.

We also covered Mardi Gras and the Southern Republican Conference, where the GOP's "southern strategy" was born. We documented the integrations of the schools in the South, the "Rap" Brown trial at the old Federal Courthouse in the French Quarter, the black power movement, and the police raids of Black Panther operations in New Orleans.

Lydia, my wife at the time, and I lived in a shotgun apartment on St. Peter Street in the French Quarter. Our apartment was like a restaurant, always somebody coming to dinner—people like the great photographer and storyteller Lyle Bongé, the playwright and writer James Kirkwood, and the writer James Leo Herlihy. I met Vernel Bagneris while he was a college student working as a waiter at the Vaucresson Restaurant on Bourbon Street. I learned about the Creole culture and particularly its cuisine. Allan Jaffee and his wife were running Preservation Hall, where some of the old musicians, well into their eighties and nineties, were still playing. I learned about New Orleans Dixieland jazz.

We lived about two blocks from Buster's Place, where a hungry body could get a plate of red beans and rice for 35 cents (75 cents with sausage). Twice a week Buster Holmes would make some of his whiskey-laden bread pudding, which was almost a meal in itself. The musicians and grand marshals with the different bands would meet at Buster's Place before going to play a funeral. Some friends introduced me to the jazz funerals, and after I'd photographed a few, people would phone to let me know when another musician had died, which meant another jazz funeral.

The photographs in this book are from several funerals, including those of George Lewis, Alcide Pavageau, Paul Barbarin, and Leon Shelly. I photographed them simply because they were a part of the life of New Orleans, with all their sadness and dignity, their pride and humility, their stillness and motion, their silence, and their rejoicing.

Someone asked me recently why I waited so long to publish this collection of photographs. Well, there's one answer. Like any good stock, the ideas for this book have been simmering for years. But the right ingredients weren't there to add to the pot. The time wasn't ripe.

The gumbo wasn't ready till now.

ACKNOWLEDGMENTS

I would like to thank my parents, Lovelace and Olita, for the stubbornness which has enabled me to live life my way, Cathy Craig for over three decades of good (if not followed) advice, Judy Newman for my first exhibit, Donald Sussman for the darkroom, my brother Ronald for financial bailouts, and Anita Touchet, Lynne Holton, Peter Yokum, and Elizabeth Burk for simply being there.

Vernel would like to thank Michael Gregory Gong for his expertise and assistance.

—LT

REJOICE
WHEN
YOU
DIE

INTRODUCTION
by
ELLIS L. MARSALIS, JR.

IN March of 1994, Daniel "Danny" Barker passed away. Danny was a guitarist and banjoist from New Orleans who had made it big in New York City with the Cab Calloway Band in the 1930s. One of his last requests before he passed was that he *not* be given a jazz funeral. Danny had witnessed jazz musicians playing for one of their own on the way to the gravesite many, many times as a youngster, only to become disenchanted with what he had seen and heard lately. Young brass band players today, unaware of and indifferent to the history and solemnity that traditionally accompanied the deceased to his final resting place, dance and prance to the beat of a different drummer. The old-time jazz funeral, like the old-time musicians themselves, is vanishing.

What, then, is a traditional New Orleans jazz funeral?

To begin at the beginning, it seems certain that the roots of jazz funerals reach back to Africa, where some societies to this day use similar processions in mourning and celebrating their departed. Those roots lay dormant, or nearly so, during the long years of African American slavery, not to gain new vigor until after the Civil War and Emancipation. Following the war, social-aid clubs and benevolent societies were established to assist the former slaves with medical bills, life insurance, and other forms of social support that would otherwise have been difficult or impossible for them to obtain. Twenty-five cents a week would ensure a member a proper burial.

Many of the clubs supported brass bands, which played for parties and weddings as well as for funerals. The brass bands flourished from the 1880s through the 1920s. In the 1930s the Great Depression severely hampered their activity, but neither their music nor the playing of it for funerals passed from the scene. Indeed, there are musicians still alive who are veterans of that time. I recently had a brief but fruitful telephone conversation with Harold "Duke" DeJan, the leader of the Olympia Brass Band. DeJan began playing with the Holy Ghost (church) Brass Band under the directorship of Pinchback Tureaud and remembers playing funerals for such social-aid clubs as the Vidalia, the San Jacinto, and the Tulane, as well as for the Jeunes Amis benevolent society. Like many older musicians, he describes the brass bands of the 1930s as having a much higher level of musicianship than the younger brass bands of today.

The rise of private insurance companies made the various social-aid and benevolent clubs virtually obsolete; although some still exist, their function is primarily in support of social activities. Yet even as the clubs faded for the most part into distant memory, the jazz funeral remained a vital part of the New Orleans black community. That this should be so says a great deal about that community and its uniqueness. Many other places had social-support clubs, and many of those clubs undoubtedly had bands. Only in New Orleans was a style of music so intertwined with daily life and death as to give not only its sound, but eventually its name, to a local funerary custom (although the term *jazz funeral* is a surprisingly late coinage, dating only to the 1930s).

Rejoice When You Die is photographer Leo Touchet's documentation of several jazz funerals. The photos were taken from 1968 to 1970 at the funeral processions of clarinetist George Lewis, bassist Alcide "Slow Drag" Pavageau, drummer Paul "T-Boy" Barbarin, and Leon "Nooney-Boy" Shelly, a member of one of the social and pleasure clubs. The time frame is important, for it was in the 1970s that jazz funerals began to change irrevocably from their traditional form. Touchet's photographs show the end of an era.

The photos represent the two main aspects of the traditional jazz funeral: the somber journey to the gravesite (Part 1) and the exuberant return from it (Part 2). They are images of a people experiencing and acting out a cultural memory that their ancestors were never allowed to express formally. In viewing them, one can almost hear the melodic strains of old Protestant hymns echoing through neighborhoods of shotgun houses and corner barrooms.

In a traditional jazz funeral, the band meets at the church or funeral parlor where the dismissal services are being conducted. After the service, the band leads the procession slowly through the neighborhood. In a recent film, *New Orleans Jazz Funerals: From the Inside,* Milton Batiste, the lead trumpeter in DeJan's Olympia Brass Band, observed that "as the procession heads through the neighborhood, you might see a black wreath hanging on the door where the deceased lived or worked." The mood is generally somber, and the musical selections are taken from Christian hymns such as "Amazing Grace" or "Just a Closer Walk with Thee" commonly sung in black Protestant churches. While playing the hymn(s), the musicians indulge in virtually no improvisation.

The distance the band walks today may be only a few blocks, since burial sites are not always within walking distance of the church or funeral parlor. If the cemetery is nearby, the band accompanies the procession to it. When the interment ceremony is completed, the band leads the procession from the gravesite without playing. When a respectful distance from the site has been reached, the lead trumpeter sounds a two-note preparatory riff to alert his fellow musicians. At this point the drummers begin to play what has become known as the "second-line" beat.

The band now sheds its solemnity in favor of music more conducive to lively, even joyous, activity on the part of family, friends, and other celebrants—the group affectionately known as the "second line." Out come umbrellas, many of them elaborately decorated, that seem to be more about styling and profiling than protection from nature's elements.

When a returning brass band is heard in the distance, that sound announces the impending arrival of a public celebration. Those who are willing and able will fall in behind the band, next to the band, between the band members, affecting the body language of a dance, a strut, a "booty bounce" to the music of the second-line beat.

One of the more popular songs of choice is "Didn't He Ramble?!" The title and the lyrics are suggestive of a free-spirited man who reaped what he had sown and had a good time doing it. Another favorite, of course, is "When the Saints Go Marching In." Legend has it that "The Saints" was a regular feature at prayer meetings and Sunday services; one day some of the churchfolk heard a jazz band playing it returning from a funeral, and it was never sung again as a part of their church services.

Playing a very important role in the brass band is the grand marshal, who may be a band member or a member of the same social or benevolent club as the deceased. His demeanor—head erect, expression solemn, dressed in a black tuxedo, white gloves, black hat held respectfully in his hand while taking slow but measured steps—is crucial to the dignity of the procession on the way to the gravesite, and his jauntiness and energy set the tone for the band and the dancing second-liners alike on the return journey that announces to the community the good news that another soul has gone on home.

Much of this has changed, or is changing, now. Although the jazz funeral is very much a part of New Orleans' black culture, some of the younger brass band players are either unfamiliar with or indifferent to the traditional music. It is common to hear bands play popular songs of the day in place of the longtime standards handed down from the older musicians, and the stately march to the gravesite is becoming a thing of the past: often now the livelier music begins at the church door. The newer bands generally are not attached to social and pleasure clubs. Moreover, whereas jazz funerals were traditionally for musicians and club members, today they are for anyone who can pay for it.

Since the 1970s, with the influence of the pop-funk music scene, brass bands like the Dirty Dozen, the Soul Rebels, Pinstripe, Algiers, ReBirth, and many other continually forming groups have carried the torch. Although the younger players do not always honor the music of the past, tradition and custom in New Orleans have themselves always been about improvising. The traditional jazz funeral expresses a recognition that there is something not only to mourn, but also to celebrate, even in death; the same truth applies to the ongoing metamorphosis of the jazz funeral custom itself.

PART 1

FUNERAL PROCESSIONS

In my short life-span, I have been referred to as "Creole" and
on to "Creole of color" then to "Colored." And who can forget
the jump up to "Negro"? "Black" was next, and a righteous
step it was. Then came "Afro-American." Now I nod my head
"uh-huh" to "African-American." The language of the "jazz funeral" has been as inclusive to its people and their times: each
generation, ever-changing, with new wounds to heal. New
voices, mindful of the traditional, name the outcries from all
of us to God's ear. From "funeral march" to "jazz funeral" to
the current "funeral with music," any name you use, a New
Orleans jazz funeral will have you experiencing something spe-
cial about the life we humans live, and the death we all face.

The low, muffled sigh of a dark old lady as she chokes

back tears, handkerchief clenched to her open, drip-

ping mouth; a dazed-eyed boy tries to maintain his

manliness, his quivering knees betraying his staunch

stance; a wife left on her own grunts trumpetlike re-

fusals of the most undeniable fact . . . death.

A son, a father, a husband. As the coffin lid locks

shut, a corpse. Friends and neighbors move into the

aisles pressing hands and cheeks, mumbling quiet

nothings. With grim finality, church bells announce

the service's end.

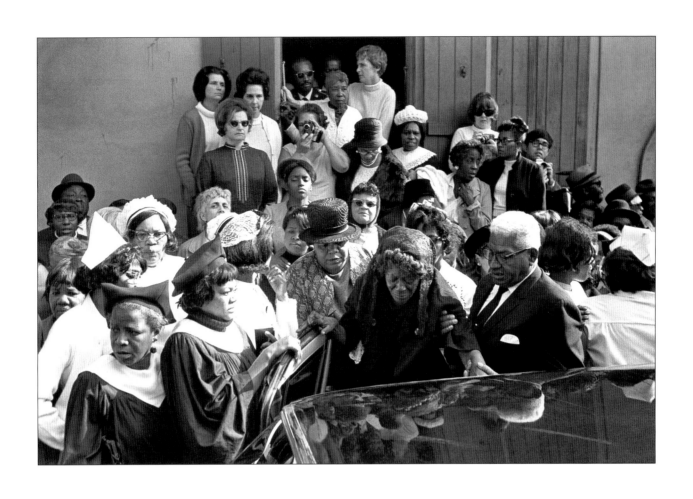

And the choir sings:

GOD BE WITH YOU

God be with you . . . (I say) God be with you

'Til we meet again.

Keep on working for the Master

Keep on singing here n'ever after

God be with you . . .

'Til we meet again.

Some things have changed in the jazz funeral over the years I'm not too happy about. The younger people have brought in more of that reggae "hop around" feeling to some of the music. I like that solid backbeat laid on the traditional march tempo. But that's me. Some things, though, I'm glad they're gone. Like those horse-drawn hearses. They were more elegant, now, don't get me wrong. But the stench from all those piles of droppings was enough to make you settle for cars. Another thing I can do without is all the fear that surrounded the funeral processions. People used to say that the soul, when first released at the graveyard, would try to invade the living persons present and take over their bodies—in short, retreating from the other world's uncertainty. So the family would shake from head to toe waddling back home. That would keep them from being easy targets. It was an eerie sight to see. In later years, drums were added to lighten the ordeal for the already burdened loved ones. Friends and lodge members, known as "second-liners," would march alongside the family offering support, protecting them from possible harassment by those with a "bone to pick": ill-tempered "other women" or rejected, illegitimate offspring. Now the "wobbling" walk in fear of possession is just part of a farewell dance from the crowd as the family releases the soul to its destiny. More instruments have been added over the years—playing spirituals and dirges when they first leave the church, then jubilant, crowd-pleasing party numbers as they toast the dead:

The soul is free . . . rejoice!

Or as we say,

"Cut 'em loose!"

And the people sing:

AMAZING GRACE

Amazing grace,

How sweet the sound, that saved a wretch like me.

I once was lost, but now I'm found.

Was blind, but now I see.

Burning sun, one hundred percent humidity, and it ain't about to rain . . . but once you hear the band coming down the block, you gotta come outside and see. I mean, it *is* right out front the house. Lawd, rest his soul and give his poor wife comforting. We were in there playing cards, and I had a lil' okra stewing on the stove. Pops! Take off your hat, baby, and show some respect. That's somebody's daddy or uncle, y'know. And one of our great New Orleans musicians, too! . . .

Low, bone-aching tempos are now pumped up with demands of release. The mandate is to mend, to heal. The pulse thickens as jazz erupts.

Hot as it is out there, I wouldn't care if it was Napoleon's funeral procession coming. I got the fan aimed right on me. So from here this'll be close enough. Misty goes crazy anyway when all that excitement starts. She bammed her head so hard last time—running and barking under the house—she almost broke my water pipes. That's all I need is having to pay the plumber again. This winter it went below freezing three days in a row. The pipes all cracked under here. I had no water for two weeks. No, I'll watch from here. I got Misty tied up to the tree out back, so y'all go ahead and carry on. I don't like to be too public nohow . . . with my business and all.

Don't set right out to change me . . . try to understand me first, that's all I'm saying.

Some of these northern priests come down here and actually won't allow a Catholic musician to have this most cherished honor bestowed upon him. Can you believe that?! No, they say it's too primitive to celebrate a man's death like we do. I guess it is . . . coming from my parents, who got it from theirs, and on down the line. Yeah, I'd say that's pretty "primitive" all right. But they try to equate it to a pagan way, insisting we should "move past it."

The grand marshal sets the tone. He wears the face of sorrow and solemnity. His dignified attire and demeanor elicit respect from the waiting crowds. His rhythmic strut, from heavy-footed marching to hopping sidesteps, will signal for all the soul's departing. It's a privileged position. Some day, I'm gonna say to one of those priests: "And by the way, Father, we have women for grand marshals nowadays, y'know. So who needs to move past it?"

Everybody sings:

C A L L   H I M   U P

Jesus on the mainline—tell Him what you want.

> *Call Him up and tell Him what you want*

> *Call Him up*

> *Call Him up*

Call Him up and tell Him what you want.

When you sick and you can't get well

> *You better tell Him what you want*

> *Call Him up*

> *Call Him up*

Call Jesus up and tell Him what you want.

Gold piece in my right palm, head resting on a silken pillow, like I was just taking an afternoon nap after some good "horizontal refreshment." Yes, how sweet it is to know you died standing pat. The boys'll make sure I'm dressed up in my finest, paraded in front of all my favorite spots before being laid to rest. Flowers decorated in shape of my instrument will adorn my "marked" grave. The end of a perfect death!

Didn't have much say so coming in, so I'm not expecting much to do with going out of this blessed life. And I do mean "blessed." Okay, I didn't have no money to speak of, but I really didn't need all that much of nothing with the kind of family and friends I knew were looking out for me. And once I understood the God-given talent that was in my hands to play an instrument?! I had it made in the shade.

PART 2

SECOND LINE

The smell of beer and sweat flavors the warm humid

air as the crowd swerves hips and thick thighs in per-

cussive response. The band, enticed to dig lower,

growls and swears in abandonment of the standard

melody line.

And the band plays:

LORD, LORD, LORD

Lord, Lord, Lord, You been so good to me

Lord, Lord, Lord, You been so good to me

Lord, Lord, Lord, You been so good to me

You saved my soul from sin and shame.

And all his boys'll sing:

DIDN'T HE RAMBLE

Didn't he ramble, Didn't he ramble

He rambled all around, in and out of town

Didn't he ramble, Didn't he ramble

He rambled 'til the butcher cut him down.

Racially, we're typical of any pirate seaport or sailor's resting spot. Lots of Spaniards and the French, mixing with the native Indians plus African slaves and "free people of color." In "The City That Care Forgot," as the locals dubbed it, this casual abandoning of the standard bloodline, so to speak, created not only a unique culture, people, and music, but a great place to live . . . and die.

That's the burial afforded the people who helped to carry the music along in New Orleans. 'Cause everybody knows the music is the key . . . the "roux." If you cook, you understand. If not, the roux is the basic seasoned stock that can take you in any direction you want to cook. Some island cultures, I've heard, keep the same roux to start out their meals for years. Every day something new added, while all the time slowly simmering. Well, that's just like our ancient customs in which we still find joy and honor.

You cry when you're born,

so rejoice when you die.

♪